With love,

Sheila.

THE HISTORY OF KNITTING PIN GAUGES

Sheila Williams

Published by

MELROSE BOOKS

An Imprint of Melrose Press Limited
St Thomas Place, Ely
Cambridgeshire
CB7 4GG, UK
www.melrosebooks.com

FIRST EDITION

Cover designed by Amanda Barrett Creative Design

ISBN 1 905226 75 6

Printed and bound in Great Britain by:
CPI Bath, Lower Bristol Road,
Bath, BA2 3BL, UK

Contents

Please note that the photographs in this book are not to scale.

Foreword

This history is confined for collecting purposes to gauges of imperial measure spanning just over a century from the 1840s to the late 1950s. As all but double-pointed needles were marked with their size and knitting 'in the round' became less popular after the Second World War, gauges became simpler, usually incorporating metric sizes, and many of the smaller manufacturers had either merged or disappeared. For the collector, the 'Golden Age' had ended.

My interest in collecting gauges began when I found that I had an assortment lurking in the bottom of work bags and boxes. For the knitter of fine Victorian patterns these are essential for sizing thin steel needles, and over the years I seem to have collected quite a few. Most were bell shaped and looked pretty similar, but close inspection revealed that their makers were different and each had a distinctive trademark. And so it began; every charity shop and flea market yielded more for my collection and I just had to know who these manufacturers were and when the gauges were made.

As with most collections it grew to be an obsession, and I began to look for information to guide me. To my great disappointment I found that, although much had been written on needlework tools, knitting was scantily covered. So I decided to search for myself, beginning at the British Library, then visiting museums and acquiring a small library of magazines and early books of my own.

The greatest problem was the disappearance of most of the archive material when the old needle mills were demolished in the 1980s and 1990s. But thanks to a dedicated band of helpers and an enlightened staff, the Forge Mill Needle Museum was established at Redditch and the remaining fragments of a once proud industry salvaged. The museum and its curator have provided me with the bones of my research.

I quickly got to know fellow collectors who were happy to share their interest with me. I am also indebted to the curators at the Birmingham Central Library and the Museum in the Park at Stroud (Glos.), The Dunstable and District Local History Society and the historian of the Manningtree Museum, all of whom have given their time to enable me to piece together the many loose ends.

I would like to give a special vote of thanks to the following collectors who have provided detailed information on manufacturing companies: Jo-Ann Gloger of the Forge Mill Needle Museum, Gay Lines and members of the Needlework Tools Collector's Society of Australia for the Australian companies, Dennis Barber for research on Cox & Co., Brian Jowett for the history of Kirby Beard and Joyce Pointer for her dedicated sleuthing.

The following collectors have given permission for items in their collections to be photographed for publication: Clarice Birch and Gay Lines (Australia); Rita Heath, Joyce Poynter and Evelyne Raphael (United Kingdom).

Author's own collection photographed by Tony Woods Photography (www.tonywoodsphotos.co.uk).

Introduction

With the spread of literacy, knitting began to cross social boundaries. The early knitting books were slim volumes for the use of ladies of leisure. From the mid 1830s writers such as Jane Gaugain, Miss Watts, Mrs Savage, Elizabeth Jackson, Cornelia Mee, Frances Lambert, Mlle Riego and many others produced drawing room books expensively priced from around 5/- for small plain editions to an exorbitant 12/6d for the illustrated versions.

Not all middle-class women were able to afford such luxury; some even had to supplement their income by knitting small saleable items for shops, and for these impoverished souls writers began to produce cheaper books such as Jane Gaugain's *The People's Book* priced at 2/6d. She produced even cheaper volumes priced at only 1/-, expressing her delight that they had been 'of much benefit to the humble class of Females'.

The great step forward in knitting came with the 1870 Education Act which gave free education to the masses. Before this, education had been given to the poor by enlightened reformers and religious bodies. The National Society's schools, established in the mid 19th century by the Church of England, stressed the importance not only of the three Rs but also saw that their pupils were given instruction in needlework and knitting so that they could earn or supplement the family income.

By the 1870s drawing room books were being superseded by cheaper periodicals which were well within the reach of the working classes. In 1870, after his wife's death, Samuel Beeton published *Beeton's Book of Needlework*, and in the 1880s the popular periodical magazines published by Weldons began to appear. Priced at just 2d they were an immediate success. An even cheaper magazine, Leach's *The Penny Knitter*, appeared in 1892.

Some of the early writers, and certainly all the later periodicals, stressed the importance of tension. It was obviously necessary to have some tool for measuring the needle sizes and gradually gauges based on the contemporary engineering wire gauges began to appear.

By this time most of the well-known needle-making enterprises were already established in or around the Redditch area. The advent of steam power had allowed the various manufacturing processes such as pointing, hardening and scouring to be brought together in what were to become factories where work could be carried out in one management complex. The age of mass production was under way.

It is at this time that the names so eagerly sought by today's collectors emerged as leaders in the field.

Names such as Morrall, Milward, Hall, Bartleet, Walker, Woodfield, Lewis & Baylis, Smith, Shrimpton and Critchley were all to leave their mark on the industry and provide the tools to satisfy the burgeoning interest in the craft of knitting.

The Introduction of
Trademarks in the
19th Century

As companies grew it became necessary that they identify their products in an easily recognised way. Foreign markets were opening up, and here in Britain in the mid 19th century the working classes were largely illiterate. A form of pictorial identification, or trademark, not only identified the maker, but also gave the buyer confidence in the product.

Trademarks became the seal of respectability. Companies searched for family crests and registered a veritable menagerie of beasts and birds to emblazon needle wrappers and metal accessories such as knitting pin gauges. A simple bell gauge, for instance, carries a wealth of information from the number of needle sizes to the manufacturer's or retailer's mark stamped boldly on each small piece of metal.

Here proud griffins compete with elephants, ostriches, foxes, peacocks, ducks, bees, archers, scimitars, cornucopias, crosses, crowns and even royal coats of arms. Trace the history of these marks and you are into the world of 19th century industry and enterprise.

Collecting and Dating Gauges

Dating a gauge can be very difficult. Trade catalogues, where they exist, show that designs often remained the same for decades, but there are some indications that can help the collector.

As a rule of thumb, the greater the number of needle sizes the older the gauge. The first bell gauge, for instance, has 28 sizes, reflecting the Victorian interest in fine knitting and crochet. As the 20th century progressed, however, fine work lost popularity and the smaller sizes began to disappear from the gauges. When chunky yarns were introduced in the 1950s, 00 and 000 sizes were added. In the late 1950s companies such as Abel Morrall and Henry Milward began to incorporate metric sizes in anticipation of metrication – in the case of knitting needles this took place in 1975.

It must be borne in mind, however, that both the Morrall's Griffin and the Milward's /Archer bell gauges kept their 24 sizes well into the 1930s.

The finish of a gauge can give some idea of age, even if a rather negative one. Ivory, bone and wood were used for many of the earliest gauges, for instance, Frances Lambert's '*filière*', which is believed to be the first gauge ever made, is an ivory disc. However, these natural substances were quickly superseded by metal. Not only was it more robust, but it was also easier to pierce accurately with the calibration.

There is mention in mid 19th century books and trade catalogues of 'polished zinc' and 'white metal' (which was probably also zinc), but brass was the favoured metal. It did not rust and could be used alone or plated. Apart from some rare early examples of silver plating on copper, such as George Chamber's bell gauge (1847) and George Curling Hope's Cornucopia (1848), brass gauges were plated with nickel. This substance was identified in the mid 18th century and was used, after the commercial development of electroplating around 1840, to plate base metal. It was an ideal substance for plating knitting pins and gauges for it is particularly resistant to corrosion. By the 1870s most gauges were being offered in nickel-plated brass.

Cheaper chromium plate was not in general use until the mid 1920s, but infuriatingly for the collector most companies continued to use the more expensive nickel because of its quality. It does, however, date chromium-plated gauges as post-1925. At this time steel was also used for the production of gauges and this is invariably chromed. The presence of steel is easily detected using a magnet.

Some 20th century gauges used a relatively new metal alloy – duralumin. This was developed around

1910 by Alfred Wilm, a German metallurgist. By mixing aluminium with other metals such as copper and magnesium he obtained a strong alloy which kept the lightness of aluminium while giving greater strength. It was much used for aircraft during WWI, and companies such as Jarrett & Rainsford of Birmingham which had made use of the metal for war work soon found that it was ideal for their haberdashery trade (see below under the heading Stratton & Co. (Stratnoid)).

Much used for knitting pins, duralumin had one big problem, it rubbed off with use, soiling the yarn. In 1923 the first anodising process in England was used, primarily for the protection of seaplanes. Colourful coatings were developed for many decorative articles, including knitting pins and a few gauges such as those made for Emu (see below under the heading Yarn Spinners and their Gauges). In 1933, Morralls developed their Aero grey coating which was more durable for both gauges and pins.

As technology advanced in the 19th century, new developments produced a group of 'plastic' materials which were quickly taken up by knitting pin makers. Vulcanite (1839) and celluloid (1862) were ideal substances for knitting needles and crochet hooks but only rarely used for gauges, the exceptions being small rules and bookmarks of the 1930s (see below under the heading Measures).

The first plastic to be used for gauges was Bakelite. It was developed in 1907 by Leo Baekeland, a Belgian-born chemist working in the United States of America. By heating phenol (derived from coal tar) and formaldehyde he obtained a thermo-setting resin which could be pressure moulded into a multitude of rigid shapes.

Early Bakelite was limited in colour to dark shades of red, blue, green and brown, usually mottled in appearance. In the mid 1920s, lighter, delicately mottled Bakelite was achieved by substituting thiourea for the phenol, which in turn was replaced by urea to give urea formaldehyde. By the end of the 1920s, light, clean colours were possible. Typical examples of the use of Bakelite are gauges made for Patons in Australia and those incorporated in knitting pin boxes and wool holders (see below under that heading).

A material much used for knitting pins and some colourful gauges was casein. It is a substance made from milk solids (curds as opposed to whey). When hardened in formaldehyde it can be extruded as rods and sheets. It was first patented in Germany in 1899 under the brand name of Galalith.

In 1909 a company was set up in Stroud, Gloucestershire, to manufacture a casein product which they named Syrolit. The process used was not successful, however, and the company was bankrupt by 1913. A new company was formed in the same premises, and using the German method of manufacture, a successful product called Erinoid was produced. At the commencement of WWI, Erinoid Plastics filled the gap left by the German manufacturers and they were to remain the major producer of casein plastics in the United Kingdom until the 1980s.

It was an ideal substance for the manufacture of knitting pins, and a whole range appeared to delight the knitters of the interwar period. Manufacturers such as Charles Horner of Halifax used casein for a huge range of haberdashery goods, among them knitting needles and gauges for Patons & Baldwins (see below under the heading Yarn Spinners and their Gauges).

Identifying plastics can be difficult, but a few simple tests can be done. All knitters know that vulcanite is black and smells of burnt rubber when rubbed hard; similarly, celluloid gives off a faint smell of camphor. But the collector of gauges has a more difficult task as Bakelite, casein and petroleum-based plastics can look fairly similar.

When casein is put into hot water it will smell of sour milk (but be careful not to warp your gauges!). The hot needle test is the only reliable method for Bakelite and modern plastic. Dig the eye end of the needle into a cork and heat the point over a candle flame. Applying a little pressure, push the needle into an unobtrusive part of your gauge or box. Bakelite will be difficult to pierce and the hole will remain rigid; modern petroleum-based plastic will yield quickly and melt around the edge of the hole.

Through the 1960s and 1970s many companies merged or went out of business and by the 1980s only two remained, Abel Morrall and Henry Milward. Even their time was limited and gradually manufacture was moved abroad and many of the old mills were pulled down.

During this time gauges became more stereotyped. Rectangular gauges in aluminium and petroleum-based plastic began to take the place of the more attractive shapes and, although there are some gems for the collector, such as Milward's Braille gauge, the Golden Age disappeared with the 1950s.

Gauges and Their Makers

Before 1850

The earliest known gauges were devised by writers on knitting and crochet. In 1843 Frances Lambert stated in *My Knitting Book* that she had 'sometime since' invented a standard *filière* to gauge the size of needles and hooks. These were bone or ivory discs, engraved with her name and punched with holes sized 'according to the standard British wire gauge'.

Like so many of the early writers on needlework matters, Miss Lambert had her own emporium, firstly at 7 Conduit Street, London, and later, at the time of the publication of her book, at 3 New Burlington Street, London. She was also an embroideress to Queen Victoria.

Miss Lambert was the first writer to stress the importance of tension, although she is not too specific, stating only that knitters should work to a medium tension. She does, however, advise the use of a needle gauge, and in her book *The Handbook of Needlework*

Miss Lambert's ivory *filière*, 1842.

(published in 1842 at the then exorbitant sum of 9/6d) she illustrates both an industrial gauge, as used by wire drawers, and her own 'Standard Filière'. She confidently insists that 'the discrepancy as to the size of needles … will in future be obviated'.

Unfortunately, her standard differed from that of other writers, and as George Curling Hope on introducing his own gauge in 1848 points out, his calibration conformed to all other gauges except that of Miss Lambert!

Another prolific writer on knitting was Cornelia Mee. She and her husband had a needlework emporium at 41 Milsom Street, Bath. It was from here in 1842 that she published her *Manual of Knitting, Netting and Crochet.* In this she illustrates her own knitting pin and crochet hook gauge. It is a small metal disc, inscribed with her name and address in Bath. Its sizes, 10–26, show her interest in crochet which she claims to have invented, a distinction she has to share with Mlle Riego. In fact

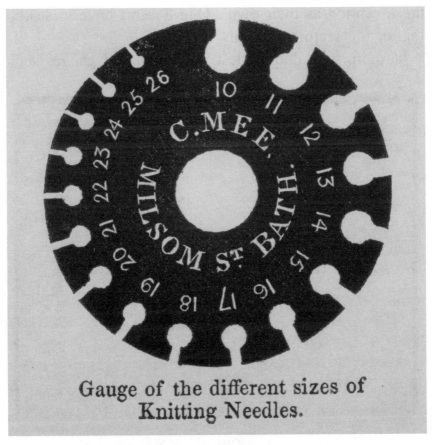

Cornelia Mee's steel gauging disc, 1842.

a form of crochet had been practised in England in the 18th century but was acknowledged, according to the title page of one of Mrs Mee's later books, merely as 'common shepherd's crook knitting'.

Other needlework writers soon began to offer their own versions of the knitting pin gauge. Elizabeth Jackson writing in the 1845 edition of *The Practical Companion to the Work Table* states that some writers 'have asserted that no standard measure exists; whilst others, with equal truth but less modesty have claimed the invention as their own'. One doesn't have to search far for the recipient of this barb!

Jackson, with due modesty, explains that gauges such

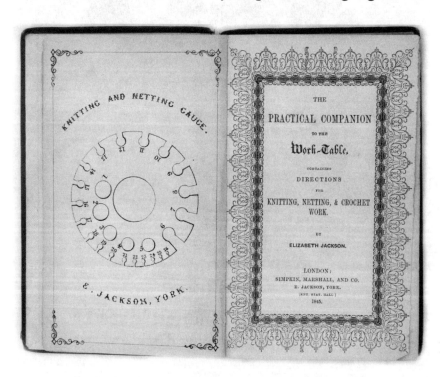

Elizabeth Jackson's steel disc-shaped gauge, 1845.

as the one illustrated in her volume had been in use by wire drawers for centuries and 'may be relied on for its perfect accuracy'. She describes it as a circular piece of steel beautifully finished. It has 26 needle sizes.

To be fair to Frances Lambert, at that time wire gauges could differ. The Standard Wire Gauge (SWG) was not legalised until 1893, and the Birmingham Wire Gauge (BG) not until 1914. Professional rivalry was probably as keen in the knitting business as it was in most trades.

Another early writer was Mrs Savage who, with her husband William, opened a needlework shop in Winchester in 1836. They later moved from these small premises in The Square to a larger emporium in the High Street where they expanded the business to include souvenir china.

On being plied with questions as to which of the confusing types of gauges was the most suitable, Mrs Savage in the 1846 edition of her *Winchester Fancy Needlework Instructor & Manual of the Fashionable & Elegant Accomplishment of Knitting & Crochet* advises her own gauge, a beautiful crescent-shaped item with 28 sizes. It is inscribed with her monogram and 'Mrs Savage's Crescent Gauge'. She states boldly that 'the numbers on this gauge are the same as those from which all knitting pins, netting meshes and crochet hooks are manufactured'. The German silver version (also known as nickel silver) was priced at 1/- and a cheaper 'mosaic gold' at 9d.

In 1848 the Curling Hopes introduced their own

Two Standard
Wire Gauges
similar to
those used
by engineers
and needle
makers.

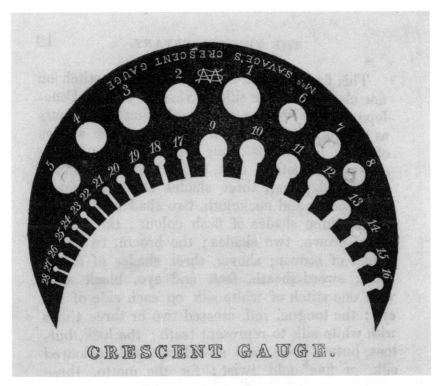

Mrs Savage's German silver Crescent, 1846.

gauge. The couple were prolific writers on all aspects of knitting, needlework and crochet. Mrs Hope ran a needlework shop at 58 Queen Street in Ramsgate. As this was a very popular seaside resort in Victorian times it was, no doubt, frequented by ladies of leisure taking the sea air. For those who could not visit, they ran a mail order service.

They called their gauge the Cornucopia, making its shape that of a shell. An advertisement in Mrs Hope's booklet *The Knitter's Friend* indicates that it came in silver plate and polished zinc, priced 1/- and 8d respectively. In both qualities it is a rare find. In 1865

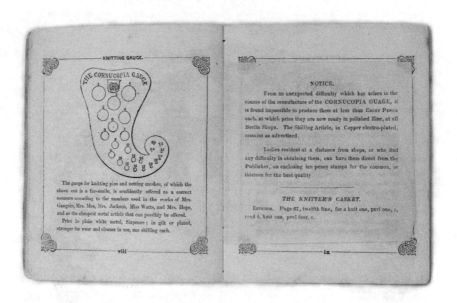

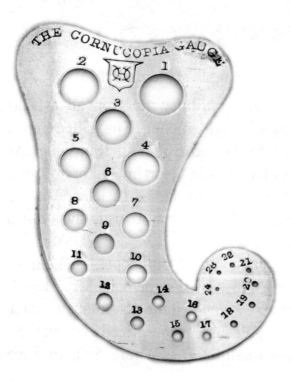

The Curling Hope's
Cornucopia gauge,
silver plate on
copper.

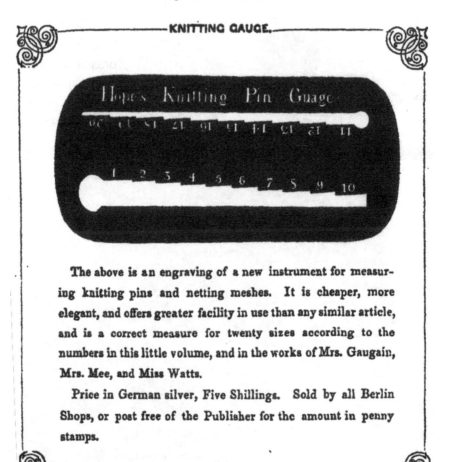

The above is an engraving of a new instrument for measuring knitting pins and netting meshes. It is cheaper, more elegant, and offers greater facility in use than any similar article, and is a correct measure for twenty sizes according to the numbers in this little volume, and in the works of Mrs. Gaugain, Mrs. Mee, and Miss Watts.

Price in German silver, Five Shillings. Sold by all Berlin Shops, or post free of the Publisher for the amount in penny stamps.

viii

Illustration from the 1865 edition of Hope's *Knitter's Friend*.

the couple offered a 'cheaper, more elegant' rectangular gauge with slot calibration. At a price of 5/- one assumes that prices had risen considerably in 17 years! This is also rare.

All these gauges were made for writers of needlework books, but in 1847 George Chambers, a leading needle maker based at the Priory Mills in Studley, patented and

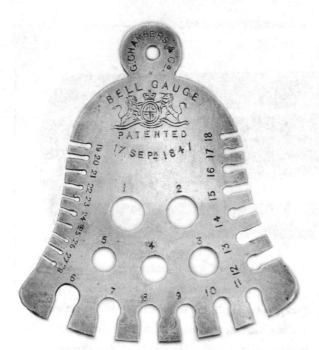

George Chamber's 1847 brass bell gauge showing the Royal Coat of Arms.

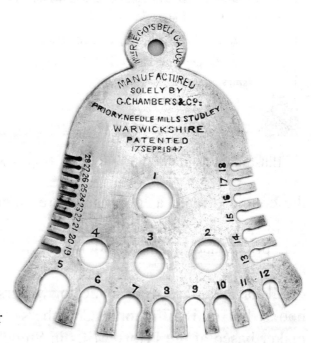

Chamber's bell gauge made for Mlle Riego. Silver plate on copper.

made the first bell-shaped gauge. Some are brass, others silver plated on copper; all are clearly marked with the factory name and patent, some displaying the Royal Coat of Arms, others with the words 'Mlle Riego's Bell Gauge' stamped around the ring.

Mlle Riego de la Branchardière was a prolific writer on needlework and may have been the inspiration behind this beautiful and rare gauge. She had royal commissions for her needlework and won numerous gold medals, particularly for crochet work which she popularised. Crochet had been known in Britain as early as the 18th century when it was known as 'shepherd's crook knitting' but lost popularity until the Victorian period.

Although the arrangement of the Chambers' gauge differs from later examples in that its calibration is rather cramped along the lower sides, it was to become the standard shape for most subsequent gauges for almost 100 years. The choice of a bell shape is intriguing, but may have been based on simple economics – as any pastry maker will know! The shape, if placed alternately upright and upside down, is easily stamped out with very little waste and also offers more peripheral space for slots.

Apart from these two variations, Chambers' gauges are fairly similar. This was probably because of financial difficulties experienced in the years prior to George's death in 1865. The following year his estate came under the administration of creditors and the company name disappeared from local directories shortly afterwards.

Gauges After 1850

As the interest in knitting grew, many small local manufacturers began to make gauges, usually in natural substances such as bone, ivory, card or wood. These were often part of a travelling pedlar's pack such as the two illustrated gauges, one resembling a tapering ivory collar stiffener, the other a plain bone oblong. Other examples, not illustrated, are: a wooden gauge marked 'The Lion and Leopard', a globe of vegetable ivory (coquilla nut shell) pierced with 20 sizes, and a miraculously preserved specimen made of prettily decorated pink card. There must be many of these early anonymously made gauges waiting to be found.

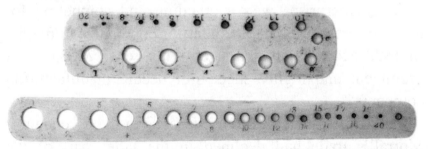

Local craftsman-made ivory/bone gauges, typical of
a pedlar's ware.

By the 1870s knitters were not only supplied with cheap patterns but also with durable metal gauges mass-produced by the major needle-making companies. Many of these companies were to remain household names for almost a century.

Abel Morrall

One of the most interesting gauge and needle makers is Abel Morrall. His gauges show more clearly than any others the development and history of a company.

The Morrall history as needle makers dates back at least to the 18th century when brothers Abel and Michael were on record as working at the Washford and Ragley Mills. In 1861 Morralls registered their Griffin trademark at Stationers' Hall. This mark, based on the family crest of a demi-griffin, appears on all Morrall bell gauges with the exception of their Aero brand bells launched in 1933.

With the development of steam power and the arrival of the railway in the 19th century the Redditch needle-making enterprises were expanding and competing for trade. It often became expedient for companies to merge. In 1898 Morralls amalgamated with Lewis & Baylis, a prominent and highly successful needle manufacturing company.

Just as the Lewis & Baylis star was in the ascendancy, Morrall's trade had declined in the latter part of the 19th century. However, the Morrall name and Griffin trademark were well-regarded assets and it was agreed that it would be in the interests of both companies to merge under the Morrall name.

A descendant of the original Abel, Colonel Morrall, became the chairman of the amalgamated companies, remaining in that position for 40 years. The running of the company, however, was firmly in the hands of the Lewis family who expanded the business to include many haberdashery items. Extra warehousing was acquired in London and Manchester, and in 1929 a central warehouse was established in Redditch.

In the absence of early trade catalogues it is difficult to date the very first Griffin gauge, but it is likely, as the introduction of the standard bell was a radical change, that the earlier Ace of Spades-shaped brass gauge, was

Abel Morrall's early
brass Griffin gauge,
late 19th century.

made well before the merger. Here a large griffin sits under three central calibration holes with the rest of the 24 sizes spaced around the perimeter. Few examples of this gauge exist, making it a collector's gem.

The best known and the most frequently found of the Griffin gauges is bell shaped, again with 24 sizes. They are usually found in nickel-plated brass. For the observant collector there are a few variations such as the aberrant spelling of 'guage' – not an uncommon spelling in Victorian and Edwardian days. This seems to have been rectified on the later examples. The sizing is made by putting the needle into the round part of the outer slots and pulling it through the narrower exit. I have termed this the 'pull through' type.

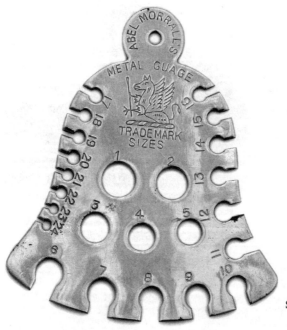

Morrall's nickel-plated bell 'guage'. This aberrant spelling was rectified on later examples.

The next stage in the development of the Griffin bell came in the early 1930s with the addition of a 1″ tension slot.

This new shape has a registered number of 804915. The gauge slots are parallel sided and there are only 18, reflecting the change to thicker yarns. The earlier and less common of these were made in nickel-plated brass and bear the Griffin trademark, but these soon gave way to the well-known Aero brand. However, the standard Griffin bell with 24 sizes continued to be offered in trade catalogues until the late 1930s.

The Abel Morrall company developed the Aero range and registered the trademark in 1933. To keep up with modern developments and to match their Aero brand

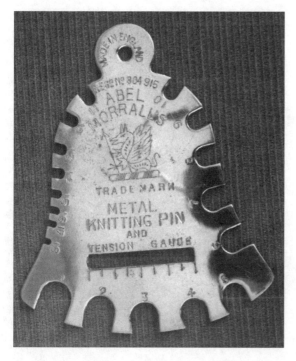

Morrall's new shape, registered as 804915 in the 1930s. Nickel-plated brass.

Morrall's Aero bell displaying the Lewis & Baylis Cross Fox trademark. Anodised aluminium.

Morrall's Aero trademark was registered in 1933.

knitting pins, these gauges were made of anodised aluminium alloy in the familiar grey colour. The earlier examples have the Cross Fox trademark, which Lewis & Baylis had brought to the amalgamation in 1898; a later version used the Aero name alone. However, trade catalogues show both versions throughout the 1930s, but the collector will find the Cross Fox brand less plentiful.

One of the shortest-lived of Morrall's gauges bears reference to the above amalgamation. Lewis & Baylis owned the Clive Works in Redditch and the Clive name was used as a trademark on a number of Morrall's sewing and knitting tools. The Clive gauge is a small rectangle in Erinoid – a casein product produced by Erinoid Plastics based at Stroud (Glos.). It is typical of the interwar period when new plastics featured strongly in the knitting pin industry. The Clive gauge was

KNITTING PIN GAUGES

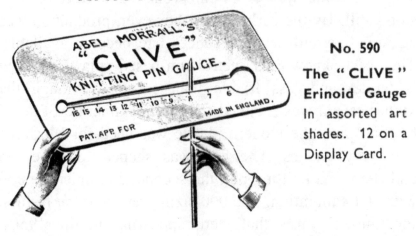

No. 590

The " CLIVE "
Erinoid Gauge
In assorted art
shades. 12 on a
Display Card.

Advertisement from one of Morrall's 1930s' trade catalogues.

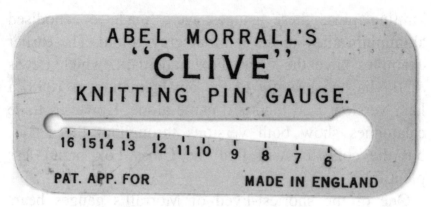

Morrall's Erinoid (casein) gauge.

advertised in 'assorted art shades'. Its calibration is in the form of a tapering slot with dumb-bell ends and its relatively short period of manufacture makes it a rare gauge.

In a 1930s' trade catalogue Morralls offered a small celluloid register, the 'Jesco Knit Glyde' which incorporated a gauge (see below under the heading Registers).

In 1939 the war years intervened and development stood still. By the early 1950s, however, production was again active and new substances had become available. The best known is petroleum-based plastic which is harder and less friable than casein. Although the kinder casein was retained for the manufacture of some knitting pins, the modern plastic was used for Morrall's new grey gauges. The first was shaped like the top and stem of a knitting pin, the second, a simpler version with slot calibration. The 000 sizing reflected the fashion for 'jumbo' yarns that were appearing in the 1950s. Also, in anticipation of the change to metric sizing,

Early 1950s' plastic gauge incorporating metric sizes.

Later version of Morrall's Imperial/Metric gauge.

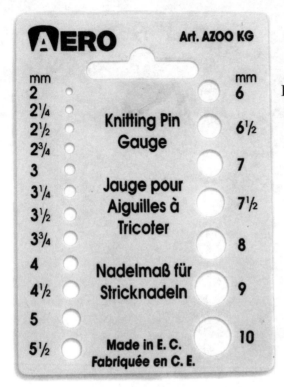

Modern Aero gauge after the acquisition of the trademark by the German company Rump & Prym in 1995.

metric numbers appeared on the reverse side (knitting pins did not become metric until 1975). A rare yellow version of the earlier gauge has been identified in Australia.

In 1983 Morralls became part of the Needle Industries together with firms such as Milwards. In 1995 the Aero trademark was assigned to the German company Rump & Prym. The Aero trademark appears on a modern rectangular gauge made by this company.

Henry Walker

The name of Henry Walker was well-known to Victorian needlewomen. Many contemporary publications such as *The Young Ladies' Complete Guide to the Worktable* recommended Walker's metal bell gauge which could be purchased at good haberdashers or at Walker's own warehouse (the name then given to a large store) in Gresham Street, London.

An 1874 trade catalogue lists, as well as the bell, slim, parallel-sided gauges in ivory, bone and boxwood. These are D-ended and have 20 needle sizes. Possibly because the metal bells were preferred for their durability, these gauges are rare.

Before Henry Walker's death in 1876 his bell gauges carried the Royal Coat of Arms, indicating royal patronage. These gauges have 24 needle sizes and the edge calibration of the pull through type. In the 1874

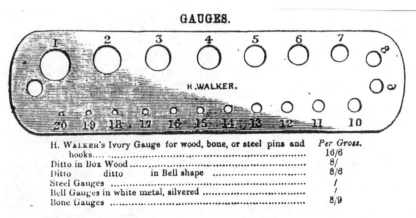

Illustration from Walker's 1874 trade catalogue showing an ivory gauge.

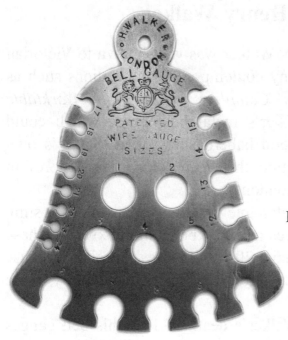

Henry Walker's brass bell gauge showing his Royal Warrant. The Royal Coat of Arms disappeared after Walker's death in 1876.

The Henry Walker gauge after 1876 displaying Barleet's Archer trademark. After a further transfer to Milwards in 1904, the words 'The Archer' also appear just beneath the ring. Both versions are nickel plated on brass.

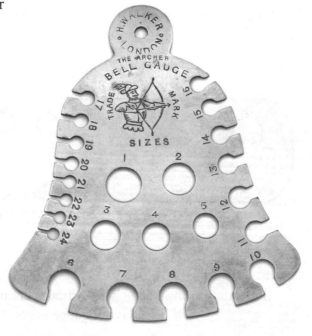

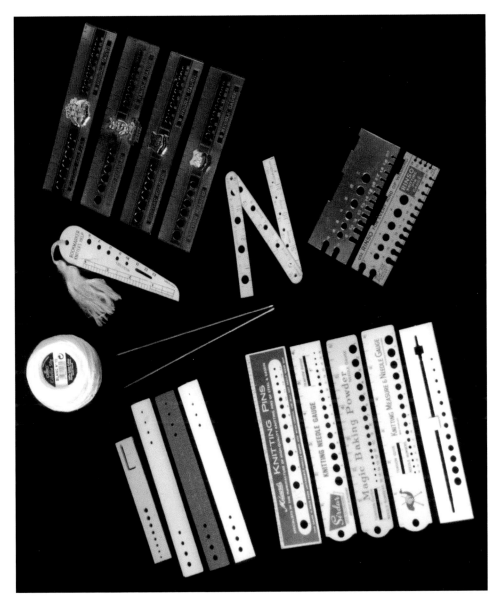

Rules and Measures *(Colour plate 1)*

Clockwise from the ball of yarn:

1. *Celluloid bookmark, measure and gauge. 1930s.*
2. *A group of metal rules with town crests or emblems. They were probably seaside souvenirs. Inter war period.*
3. *MP Handy Guide "sock and glove measure". This is found in card and thin casein. Inter War.*
4. *Two gauges of identical configuration; the first (unbranded) in heavy brass. The second, in cheap tin plate, was a free gift with Rinso washing powder. 1930s.*
5. *Petroleum based plastic rule and row counter issued free with The People's Friend. 1950s/60s.*
6. *Three celluloid rules issued as free gifts. 1930s.*
7. *Card gauge and measure advertising Milwards 'Gold Seal' knitting pins. 1930s.*
8. *A group of free gifts from Betterware. Casein, 1930s.*

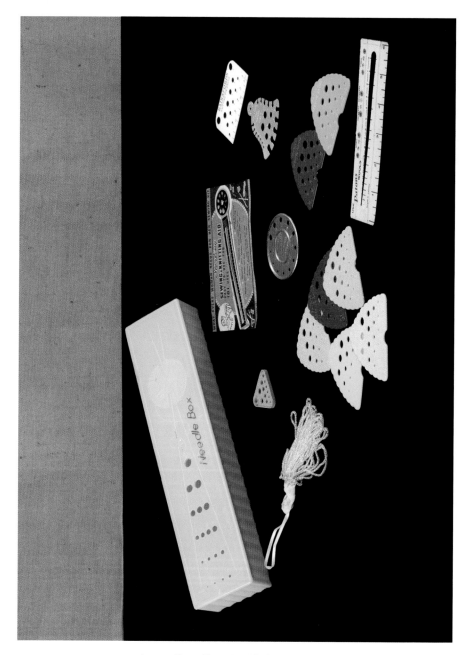

Australian Gauges *(Colour plate 2)*

1. *Lime green knitting needle box by Continental plastics, Pty. Ltd. 1950s/60s.*
2. *Beneath box – small casein triangular gauge marked 'Garnite', by Australian Consolidated Industries. 1940/50s.*
3. *To the right of No 2 – aluminium sewing aid and gauge by Sterling Steel Products, Sydney. 1950s*
4. *Beneath No 3 – a lid of a 'Keepair' knitting needle cylinder. 1940s/50s.*
5. *To the right of No 2 – Rainsford's plastic gauge. 1950s/60s.*
6. *Beneath No 5 – Rainsford's bell gauge in anodised aluminium. From 1930s.*
7. *Beneath No 6 – two Paton's Bakelite gauges showing 'Use Paton's Knitting Wools' in small capitals to base.*

Yarn Spinners and Wholesalers *(Colour plate 3)*

1. Centre Group – three casein 'beehives' made for Patons & Baldwins by Charles Horner, Halifax. This series was designed in the 1950s by Mary Gregory.

Clockwise from top right

2. A group of drum shaped gauges made for Viyella. Some with Mabel Lucy Atwell children at play. 1930s.
3. Anodised aluminium gauges supplied by Emu yarns. 1930s.
4. Nickel plated bell made by Morralls for Faudels, suppliers of 'Peacock' brand knitting wools. It shows a displaying peacock. 1920s/30s.
5. Triangular nickel plated gauge marked 'Embassy'. 1930s.
6. Nickel plated bell made by Morralls for Pearsall's silk yarns showing their 'Drake' trademark. 1920s/30s.
7. Anodised aluminium 'beehive' probably made to commemorate the tenth anniversary of the Patons/Baldwins 1920s amalgamation.
8. A group of Patons & Baldwins casein 'beehives' most probably manufactured by Charles Horner, Halifax. 1930s-50s. There is also a nickel plated version of this size.
9. The first 'beehive' issued by Patons & Baldwins in the 1920s. Nickel plated brass.

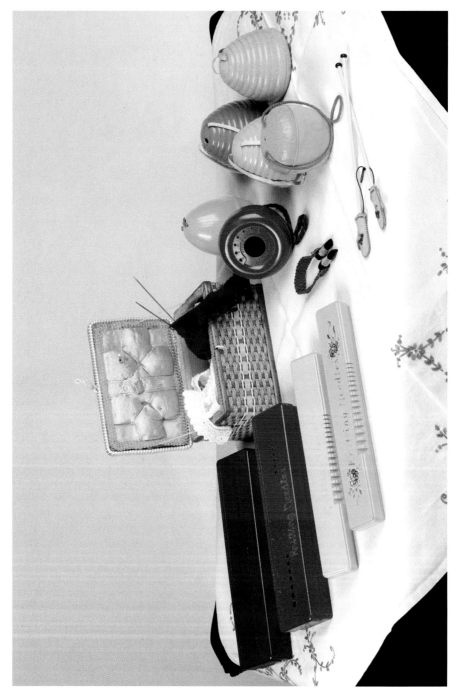

Wool Ball Holders and Knitting Pin Boxes *(Colour plate 4)*

Clockwise from work box

1. Green acorn shaped Bakelite wool ball holder made by U-Plas. Gauge to the underside. 1930s-50s.

2. Four Bakelite NB Ware holders, red holder showing the underside. The company had the permission of Patons & Baldwins to use the beehive shape. 1930s-50s.

3. Four Bakelite boxes made by Bex. Darker colours are of the earlier date. 1930s-50s

trade catalogue they are offered in 'silvered metal', which was most probably nickel plate, taking the trade price of 8/6d a gross into account. Examples have been found in plain brass. Both versions are fairly rare.

On Henry Walker's death the business was inherited by his daughter and sold to another Redditch needle maker, Robert Smith Bartleet (trading as Bartleet and Sons) for £1,100. Bartleet's trademark of an archer began to appear on the Walker gauge, but the Walker name around the ring and the calibration were kept.

In 1904 the firm of Henry Milward bought out Bartleets and the right to use the Walker name and the Archer trademark. The Walker/Archer bell was so well respected that it remained more or less the same. There is, however, one small difference in that the words 'The Archer' appear just beneath the ring. Contemporary Milward trade catalogues clearly show examples with the Archer name, dating them firmly in the Milward period. These are the most commonly found bells today.

Henry Milward

The company of Henry Milward & Sons was established in 1730 and was one of the leading needle-making establishments in the Redditch area. Work was carried out at a number of small outlying mills, but around 1850, new mills were set up in Redditch, taking the name 'Washford' after one of the earlier 18th century mills.

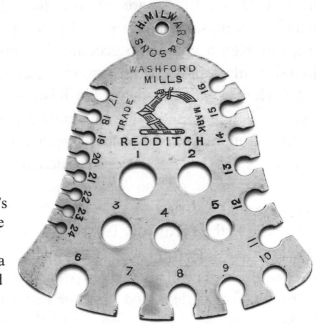

Henry Milward's brass bell gauge showing the family crest of a mailed arm and scimitar. Late 19th century.

The family crest of a mailed arm wielding a scimitar was used as a trademark for many of their sewing and knitting tools. It appears on a fairly rare nickel-plated bell gauge which seems to have given way to the Walker/Archer gauge after the takeover of Bartleets in 1904.

Milwards continued to supply the Walker/Archer gauge until the beginning of WWII, making the dating of these difficult. Even the introduction of chromium plating in the 1920s is of little use as a guide, as many companies continued to plate with nickel in spite of the process being more expensive.

In the 20th century, Milwards bought out the companies of Kirby Beard and William Hall but kept their well-known names and trademarks (see below under the company names).

After WWII it was decided to bring all the works together into new modern buildings close by the River Arrow at Studley. A competition was organised to choose the name and 'The Arrow Works' was the popular choice. The completed buildings were formally opened in 1952.

Milwards together with Morralls became part of the Needle Industries in 1983. The Milward name did not disappear, however, when the British mills finally closed. Ironically, it was the satellite companies set up in India by Milwards after WWII to cope with increased demand that finally captured all the trade. The Indian

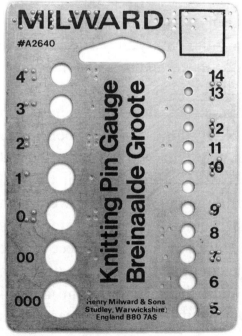

A modern Milward anodised-aluminium gauge with Braille numbering.

companies now trade under the 'Pony' name, retaining the old company name on some of their gauges.

With the move towards metrication, Milwards began to make rectangular gauges in aluminium and plastic which remain in a similar form today. For the dedicated collector the slight variations are in colour, and there is even a Braille version.

William Hall

When William Hall, the founder, died in 1851 his son-in-law, John Morgan, took over the firm. In due course the business was inherited by two of his sons, John born in 1858, and George Chambers Morgan who was born within a few months of the death of George Chambers in 1865, to whom the family were related by marriage. By the early years of the 20th century they had absorbed more than 20 needle-making companies, making them one of the giants of the industry.

The company was first based at a public house in Studley called The Fleece. In the early days, before the development of the factory system, work was carried out as a cottage industry, the workers bringing their finished goods to a central collecting point where they were paid – a pub being a popular choice! When a factory was established later in the 19th century the 'Fleece' name was kept. The company continued under the direction of the Morgan brothers until their deaths, John in 1904 and George in 1918. During the following years Halls worked closely with Milwards and the two companies amalgamated in 1930.

This date was also Milward's bicentenary and called for a great celebration. The directors of the two companies marked the occasion with a lunch catered by a local firm at 5/6d per head – a princely sum in those days. The workers were treated to a day's outing at 7/6d a head, which speaks well of management/staff relations!

After such mergers it was common practice for companies to keep their trademarks. Hall's trademark was an elephant – in heraldic terms a sign of power and strength – but it is unlikely that they produced their own bell gauge, for in all other respects it is identical to the Milward/Walker/Archer gauge. It is not a common gauge and a good find for the collector.

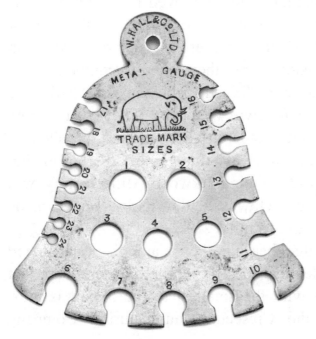

A Milward-made gauge bearing Hall's Elephant trademark. The two companies merged in 1930. Nickel-plated brass.

Kirby Beard

The Kirby Beard company has its origins in Gloucester when in 1743 a William Cowcher set up as a pin maker. In 1803 Robert Kirby joined the business, followed in 1810 by George Beard. In 1823 the company was trading under the name of Cowcher, Kirby & Beard with premises in Gloucestershire, London and Reading.

In 1840 the name of Kirby Beard & Co. was adopted, and in 1849 the company opened a needle factory at Long Crendon. A few years later the company was selling its wares in Paris and had opened a new factory, the Ravenshurst works, in Birmingham.

Sadly, at this time, competition was so great in the needle and pin trade that companies began to fail. Many of the Long Crendon workers moved to Redditch in the belief that to be at the hub of the trade would be their salvation. In 1862 they set up at Parkwood Mills in Ipsley Street, Redditch, but they failed to compete in the needle trade and were forced to buy in from Milwards and resell in their own wrappers. They were more successful with their haberdashery business, particularly with their needle cases and the famous Kirbigrip, but eventually, in 1929, their Parkwood Mills factory was sold to Milwards. However, the Kirby Beard name continued to be used until 1970.

The only gauge bearing their name is a lacquered brass oblong identical to the Crescent gauge except that the sizes begin with the smallest to the top. It is most probable that the Crescent Manufacturing Company supplied them with the gauge, which dates it similarly from the early 20th century. They are not common.

Alfred Shrimpton

John Shrimpton, born in 1651 at Long Crendon, Bucks, was the first needle maker in the family. In 1830 at least nine Shrimptons are listed as needle makers in the area, but as competition increased in the Victorian era, Alfred decided to take the risk and move to the centre of the needle-making trade in Redditch. He is first mentioned in the Redditch Directory in 1862 and two years later he was established at the Britannia Works in William Street.

Most of the Long Crendon needle makers who moved to Redditch failed. The more fortunate found work in the existing companies, but many suffered great hardship. It was Alfred Shrimpton's expertise in the manufacture of fishing hooks that gave him a well-earned place alongside the major companies. Whether he made his own gauges is doubtful for in all forms they match the Morrall die, from the earliest nickel-plated examples to the gauges with the 1″ tension slot, firstly in nickel plate and later in anodised aluminium alloy. It is also interesting to note that the registered number of the latter, 804915, is the same as the Morrall version. Shrimpton's gauges are less plentiful than Morrall's and are distinct in their inscription which shows a complex trademark of a bee, four stars, a pair of scales and two feathers. In heraldry

Shrimpton's 1930s' anodised-aluminium bell matching Morrall's 804915 registration.

The Crescent Manufacturing Company's nickel-plated brass gauge. Late Victorian.

bees signify industry and the scales may well be a pun on fish scales and their reliance on fishing hooks.

The Crescent Manufacturing Company

The Crescent works are first mentioned in the Redditch Directory in 1888, probably shortly after occupying the site of the Walton needle-making works at Mount Pleasant. It is apparent that at this time the manufactory was owned by the London-based wholesale haberdashers Olney, Amsden & Sons, as contemporary trade catalogues clearly state that they were 'the sole proprietors of the Crescent Manufacturing Company'.

Like most large concerns, Olney, Amsden had London showrooms, usually referred to as 'warehouses'. The catalogue headings show addresses at 33 Fan Street and a large warehouse comprising 9, 10 and 11 Falcon Street.

Crescent made needles, pins and knitting pins for Olney, Amsden as well as various haberdashery items, among which were two gauges. The earlier gauge, one of the most beautiful ever made, is nickel plated on brass and shaped as a crescent moon enclosing a star. Its 26 sizes indicate a Victorian date – it is a rare find.

A much simpler, lacquered brass gauge appeared in the early 20th century. It is oblong in shape with a graduated slot to the centre. Some examples are marked with the Crescent trademark and the registered number 517815, some lack the Crescent trademark and others,

Photocopy from Crescent's 1890s' trade catalogue.

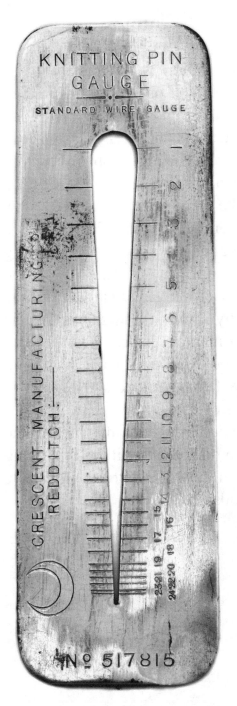

probably made for smaller companies, are unmarked. It is most likely that the Kirby Beard gauge was also made by Crescent.

The Crescent Manufacturing Company merged with Milwards in the late 1920s.

Crescent's oblong lacquered brass gauge. Early 20th century.

The Fairfax Gauge

This beautiful heart-shaped brass gauge was made for a London haberdasher called Robert Thomas Hogg (the maker is unknown). He registered the design on 19th June 1896, giving it the name of his Hampstead address of Fairfax Avenue. Having probably served his apprenticeship at the haberdashers Cox & Co., he bought the business and the premises at 99 and 101 New Oxford Street in 1865 when he was only 28. He was a man of great enterprise, gaining contracts for supplying handicraft materials and uniforms to various London boroughs. The introduction of his gauge came at a time when knitting was virtually a mania and shows that he was always in touch with market trends.

He had five daughters and three sons, some of whom, no doubt, carried on the family business. He died in 1932 at the grand old age of 95.

The Cox name was kept throughout the life of the company which was not to disappear until the rebuilding of war-torn London in the 1950s. It is interesting to note that Centrepoint now stands on the site.

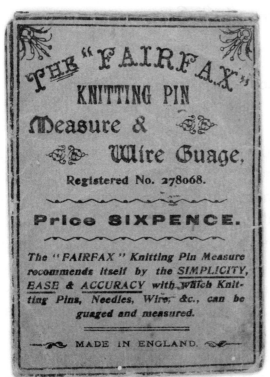

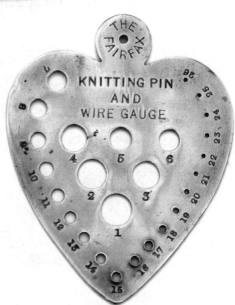

Robert Hogg's Fairfax
gauge registered in 1896
with its original packet.

Head & Son

The firm of Head & Son was a well-known haberdashery supplier with premises at 191 and 192a Sloane Street, London. They sold a huge variety of needlework goods including two metal gauges which bear their name. Both have 24 needle sizes. Their Diamond gauge was advertised 'as used by Mlle Riego' which gives it a Victorian beginning, but, like so many gauges, it was probably offered as a stock item for many years. Head's other gauge is called the Wheel of Fortune and, like the Diamond, is shaped as its name implies. Both are rare finds but the rarest must be one of Head's beautiful knitting needle cases with the gauge still in its compartment.

Sloane Street was heavily bombed during WWII and Head's premises disappeared with the post-war

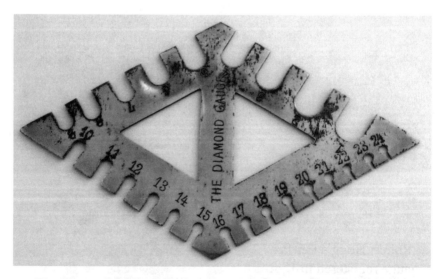

Head's steel Diamond gauge. Late Victorian/Edwardian era.

Head's steel Wheel of Fortune and its original packet.

rebuilding. The business was bought in 1952 by Clement Payne Ltd, whose premises at 24 Brompton Arcade were only a short distance away.

William Woodfield

The Woodfield company was established in Redditch in 1850. Their nickel-plated bell gauges are distinguished by the company name around the ring, a distinctively large ring hole, and their trademark of a simple cross. In the absence of trade catalogues it is difficult to date them accurately, but the 24 needle sizes indicate an early 20th century beginning when fine knitting and crochet were still popular.

Woodfield's distinctive die with its large ring hole is also evident on several other gauges. One, marked 'The Peacock', was made for Faudels, a haberdashery supplier with London premises at 36 and 40 Newgate Street. In the knitting yarn ranges Faudels offered pure silk, artificial silk (rayon) and the Squirrel and Peacock brands of wool. The Peacock name only appears on the Woodfield gauge but another Faudel gauge bearing the heraldic crest of a displaying peacock is identical to Morrall's die and was presumably made by them (illustrated on the yarn spinners colour page).

Another Woodfield gauge made and marked for a London haberdashery supplier was for Vicars of 104 Newgate Street. Other examples, for companies so far unidentified, are marked 'The Daisy', 'The Morabb', 'The Clock' and 'The Sabre'. Some are totally unmarked and were probably supplied to small companies to give away with their yarns.

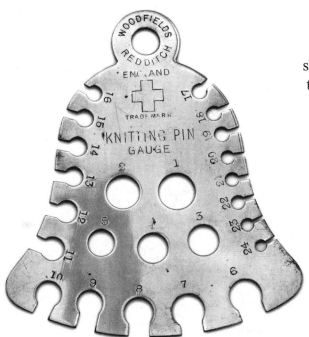

Woodfield's nickel-plated brass gauge showing the larger than average ring hole and their trademark of a simple cross. 1920s/30s.

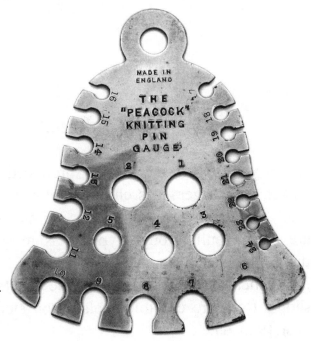

A Woodfield gauge marked 'The Peacock', the trademark of a yarn sold by Faudels.

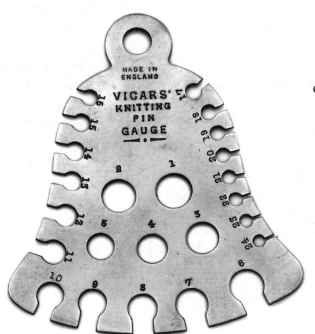

A Woodfield gauge made for the London haberdashery company, Vicars.

W. L. Jager

A fairly rare bell gauge was produced by the needle maker W.L. Jager. It is chromium plated on lightweight steel and calibrated from 0 to 24, and the outer slots are of the pull through type. It is most probable that the Ringing Bell gauge was made by Jager as the die is identical. It was possibly made for Bellman's wool shops. Both are chromium plated on steel, indicating a post-1925 date.

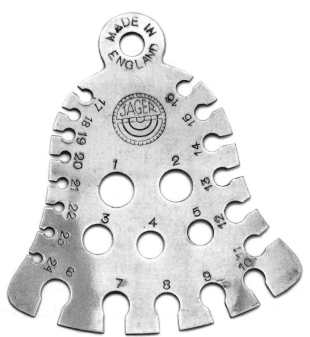

A chromium-plated steel bell made by the needle maker W. L. Jager. 1930s.

A Jager-made steel gauge showing a ringing bell, probably commissioned by Bellman's yarn shop chain.

Stratton & Co. (Stratnoid)

Stratnoid is the brand name of Stratton & Co., a company set up in 1912 by George Laughton. Its factory at the Balmoral Works, Birmingham, is best known for its fancy metal goods such as powder compacts. The Stratnoid name appears on knitting needles and gauges from the 1920s.

The company has an interesting history and close links with Australia. It has its origins in 1860 when Stephen Jarrett formed a partnership with Charles Rainsford. The company was registered as Jarrett & Rainsford, pin makers. Their products were sold to drapery and haberdashery wholesalers both in the United Kingdom and abroad.

In the 1870s Rainsford became the sole proprietor, keeping the original company name. So well did his company thrive that by the end of the century he was able to make it a private limited company with a capital of £20,000 – a great achievement in those days.

In 1898, fifteen-year-old George Laughton joined the firm. His rise was swift. In 1912 George was made a director, the managing director in 1925, and became the owner a few years later. The company was then trading as Jarrett, Rainsford and Laughton.

Due to Laughton's enterprise the Stratton company was acquired in 1912. During the coronation year of George V, Laughton was in charge of a small part of Jarrett & Rainsford which made badges and flags. Component parts were made in a small workshop owned by a man named Carter who had fallen under the influence of drink. As the work became increasingly unreliable, Laughton purchased the workshop himself for £50.

The strange choice of name came about purely as a whim of Laughton's wife who happened to be reading a novel with a hero named Stratton! It was a modest beginning for a company which was to become world famous.

At the end of WWI a new metal alloy, duralumin, came into general use. Strattons had already been using the metal for war work and decided to put it to use commercially. Laughton decided that it was an ideal material for the manufacture of knitting pins and gauges which the company began to manufacture under the brand name of Stratnoid.

There are two Stratnoid gauges, one a strange, propeller-shaped gauge which folds neatly – presumably for ease of storage. The other is an oblong D-ended aluminium gauge in both plated and anodized qualities which match the finish of the Stratnoid knitting pins. The 'propeller' dates from the interwar period and is not easily found. The oblong is of a later date and includes metric sizes.

An interesting oblong gauge, matching the shape of the Stratnoid example, was made by Colin Banks of Redditch. It is sized only in imperial measure.

When Laughton visited Australia in 1928 the company had been exporting haberdashery goods there for some time, trading through local agents. When the agents proved unsatisfactory, Laughton decided to set up his

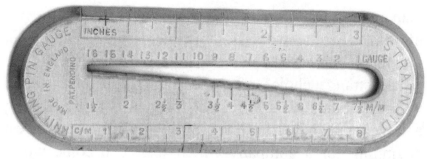

Stratnoid's oblong gauges are found in anodised and plated qualities. 1950s.

An oblong gauge by Colin Banks, Redditch, marked 'Kontrol'. This is similar to the Stratnoid example but has imperial sizes only. Gold anodised aluminium.

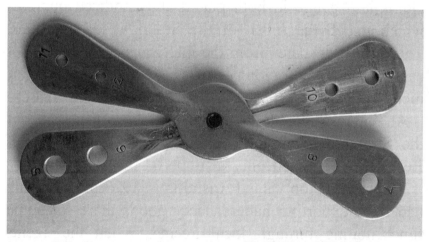

Stratnoid's propeller-shaped gauge, late 1920s/30s. Anodised duralumin.

own manufacturing company based in Sydney. He called the enterprise Rainsford Pty Ltd as a mark of respect for the founder. For further details see below under the heading Gauges made in Australia.

Wimberdar

The company name is derived from their two main mills, Wimberley Mill and Dark Mill, both situated at Brimscombe, near Stroud, Gloucestershire. The company was founded in 1883 by two brothers, Francis and Uriah Critchley, trading under the name Critchley Bros Ltd. They originally specialized in knitting pins, crochet hooks and small haberdashery items made of bone and wood.

In the 1890s the company expanded under the management of Cecil Foster Critchley, Francis's elder son. All manner of turned products were made, including hair pins, fishing rods, walking sticks and handles.

In the early years of the 20th century they began to use the revolutionary new plastic material casein, manufactured by the nearby Erinoid company. It was an ideal substance for the manufacture of knitting needles and crochet hooks as it took colours perfectly and could be marketed very cheaply.

Wimberdar disc-shaped gauges, incorporating 00 and 000 sizes, date from the 1950s when thick and jumbo yarns became popular following WWII. The most common are in plastic, so far seen in blue, yellow and green. The anodized metal versions have been found in blue, red, tan and grey. There are probably more colours in both versions. They are not uncommon, but a version marked only with the trade name of 'Coronet' is rarer. This may have been made for the haberdashery suppliers Faudels, as they marketed wools and other items under this brand name.

Wimberdar gauge marked 'The Coronet', probably made for a yarn retailer.

Wimberdar disc-shaped gauges are found in anodised aluminium and plastic qualities. 1950s.

Unattributed Gauges

There exists a small number of gauges with no manufacturer's or retailer's marks. Some, such as 'The Daisy', 'The Morabb', 'The Clock', 'The Sabre' and 'The Peacock' (made for Faudels) can be identified by their die as being of Woodfield's manufacture. A bell gauge bearing only the depiction of a ringing bell may have been made for the wool shop chain, Bellmans. It fits the die of the gauge made by the needle maker W. L. Jager, and does not match the die of other known factories.

However, some gauges have not yet been attributed to a particular maker – a nickel-plated brass bell gauge with parallel needle slots and a 1″ tension slot set vertically to the centre has no other marking. Its form suggests a 1930s' date. A heavy rectangular steel gauge is also

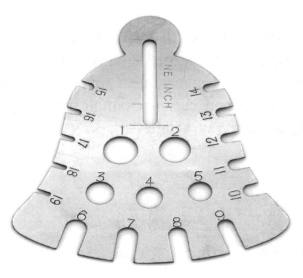

An unidentified bell in nickel-plated brass. Its sizing indicates a 1930s' date.

A post-WWII gauge in chromed steel. This is also found in cream plastic.

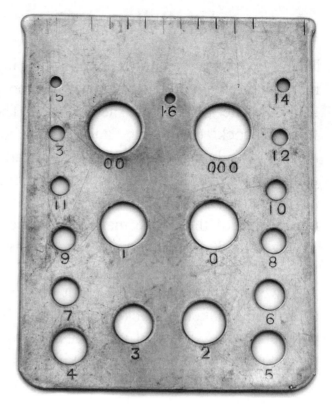

unmarked; its needle sizes are all set to the centre and, in some examples, the top edge is slightly extended to fit in a 2″ measure. This gauge is also found in cream casein. Both the metal and casein examples have 000 sizes, suggesting a post-WWII date.

Gauges Made in Australia

(For illustrations, see colour plate 2.)

Rainsford

Research has identified the location of the Rainsford factory as Sydney. They made two types of bell gauges, both using the same die with 24 needle sizes of the pull through type. One is in nickel-plated brass, the other in coated steel. They also made a rectangular plastic gauge with a 3″ measure.

The early history of the company began in England when Stephen Jarrett went into partnership with Charles Rainsford in 1860 (see above under the heading Stratton & Co. (Stratnoid)). In 1870 Rainsford purchased Jarrett's interest and widened the scope of the company. By the early 20th century the company, then known as Jarrett, Rainsford and Laughton, began exporting haberdashery goods to agents in Sydney and Melbourne.

In 1928 Laughton visited Australia with the object of disposing of the stock, the holding agents having terminated their contract. However, he was so impressed by the success of the haberdashery business that he set up a private limited company in Sydney, naming it Rainsfords Pty Ltd as a mark of respect for the company founder.

Other Australian Gauges

The craft interest in Australia encouraged many companies to produce a variety of knitting aids mostly between the 1930s and the 1950s. Sterling Steel Products of Surrey Hills, Sydney, offered an aluminium gauge and measure in a banjo shape. A rarer version of this, manufactured under the trade name of Durabel Products, has a small bell logo at the gauge end.

Australian Consolidated Industries, trading under the brand name of Garnite, made a small triangular casein gauge in a good range of colours including yellow, blue, pink and green. There are also mottled versions in green and tan. Knitters remember these being colour matched to wool ball holders.

The metal end caps of the Keepair cylindrical knitting needle cases also served as gauges. These were most probably manufactured from the 1940s in Melbourne as they are rare outside this area. The same manufacturer most probably made knitting needle cylinders for a variety of small retailers as examples of similar end caps have been found which bear no company name.

A spectacularly colourful range of Beehive gauges was made by Patons in Australia. They are as large as the original metal gauge made in the United Kingdom but the calibration is in the form of holes inside the body. They fall into two categories – the earlier 1930s' Bakelite examples have the legend 'Use Patons Knitting Wools' in small capitals at the base. The later plastic gauges have the same legend in large capitals. The colour range of these gauges gives the collector a very rich pasture with around 30 colours so far identified!

A tin plate 6″ rule incorporating a calculator was also made for Patons. (See below under the heading Measures.)

Yarn Spinners and Their Gauges

(For illustrations, see colour plate 3.)

Patons & Baldwins

The best known of all the yarn spinners is Patons & Baldwins. In 1920 J. & J. Baldwin of Halifax and Patons of Alloa amalgamated. Patons' trademark was the rose but it was the Baldwins' beehive that was to become the better known. It appeared not only on yarns but also on knitting needles and gauges, the latter always in a beehive shape.

The Beehive gauge was first mentioned in a 1920s' edition of *Woolcraft*, Patons & Baldwins' knitting manual. It is a large gauge, nickel plated on heavy brass, although some plain brass examples do exist. A slightly smaller, and rarer, version appeared later in both nickel plate and coloured casein. All these varieties have the calibration in the form of peripheral slots. Possibly made to celebrate the tenth anniversary of the amalgamation is another rare Beehive gauge in grey anodised aluminium. It shows both Patons' Rose and Baldwins' Beehive trademarks, each in a world globe.

Here the calibration is in the form of holes just inside the edge.

Recent research has shown that the firm of Charles Horner of Halifax made not only casein needles for Patons & Baldwins but also casein gauges of a small beehive shape. They were designed by Mary Gregory, Horner's talented designer, in the 1950s. They conform to the Beehive gauge shape with the sizes set evenly just inside the edge. They are to be found in a variety of colours including red, salmon, sky blue, pale blue, yellow, blush and pale green.

Viyella

Some of the most unusual gauges are those made for the Viyella company, the trade name of William Hollins of Nottingham. William Hollins began the company in 1882, manufacturing fabrics and yarns at Hollins Mill, Pleasley Vale near Mansfield.

For the knitter, Viyella offered small, enamelled-steel, drum-shaped gauges, many with delightful images of 'Mabel Lucy Atwell' children playing round the body of the drum. Other, more plainly decorated, versions are in black or green enamel with lettering picked out in gold. The calibration is found at the top of the plated steel rims, which also have stitch registers. All versions are hard to find.

Emu

Those who knitted in the 1930s will remember Emu yarns. The company, with its London headquarters at Milford House in Kirby Street, existed until the 1980s, having been for some time part of the Robert Glew and then the Thomas Ramsden groups.

The attractive anodised-aluminium bell gauges differ from the usual bells in that the calibration is within the body of the gauge. The sizes from 0 to 19 indicate a period before the chunky yarns appeared in the 1950s. So far six colours have been identified: silver, gold, blue, red, apple green and salmon pink. They are not common.

Embassy

The calibration of this fairly uncommon gauge places it in the 1930s' period. Its triangular shape is unique for a metal gauge of this date. It is chromium plated on fairly heavy steel, marked 'Standard British Wire Gauge', and sized from 5 to 20.

It is also marked 'Made in England; which possibly places its origins with R J Cole of Bingley (later of Keighley) who manufacture King Cole yarns. Some knitting pins and yarns manufactured for Coles in Australia have the Embassy trade mark, but more information is needed for the connection to be confirmed.

Pearsalls

Pearsall's silks have a long history, dating back to 1795. Their trademark of a duck or drake appears on their nickel-plated brass bell gauge which has an identical die to Morrall's Griffin gauge and was most probably made by them. It is not earlier than the 20th century as a book of patterns published by Pearsalls in 1900 recommends only Walker's bell gauge.

Sirdar

What was to become the Sirdar yarn company was founded at Ossett, Yorkshire, by brothers Tom and Henry Harrap. In 1908 Tom's son, Fred, became the sole owner, and in the 1920s he switched the company's efforts from spinning wool for machine knitting and weaving to manufacturing yarns for the hand knitting and rug wool markets. The brand name of 'Sirdar' (the title given to the Commander in Chief of the Egyptian army) was adopted in 1928 and was a reflection of Fred's admiration for Lord Kitchener. Sirdar gauges are in the form of 6″ celluloid rules (see below under the next heading).

Measures

(For illustrations, see colour plate 1.)

A small but interesting group of gauges appears in the form of rules. These date from the 1930s and were often given away by wool shops and other sales companies. The most common are the 6″ celluloid rules with a 1″ tension slot and calibration from 1 to 16. These appear to be by one maker, so far unknown, for they all agree in their calibration and appearance, differing only in the company name and the colour of the printing. The Sirdar rule, however, has the printing on the reverse side, making the tension slot to the right.

The companies which offered this type of rule are: Emu (yarns), Sirdar (yarns), WB (William Briggs of Manchester, yarns) and Magic Baking Powder (a commodity still to be found in Canada). Some unbranded examples have been found with flower decoration. The most commonly found is Emu.

The Betterware company, a door-to-door sales company specialising in home-cleaning materials, offered free gifts to their big spenders. The needle gauges appear on 6″ casein rules in a variety of colours, the most common being green, cream and red. A smaller grey rule has a pattern clip. All are calibrated from 7 to 14 and are fairly easy to find.

A blue and white 6″ cardboard rule, calibrated from 1 to 14, was issued by Milwards to advertise their Gold Seal sewing needles. Because of its fragility it is uncommon.

Patons of Australia issued a cream-painted 6″ tin plate rule with stitch and row registers to the top, activated by small wheels at the back. Its appearance suggests an early 1930s' date. It is a rare find.

A rare orange and yellow tin-plate gauge was produced for the manufacturers of Rinso washing powder. The needles sizes are from 1 to 24 which, together with its material, indicates an early 1930s' date. It incorporates a hemming measure at the top. There is also an unmarked brass gauge of identical shape.

Collectors will often find needle gauges incorporated in giftware products such as bookmarks. These are usually made of celluloid or thin casein, giving them an interwar date.

An interesting group of 6″ rules are those bearing town crests, many probably in the collections of devotees of crested ware. They are made of non-ferrous metal, some chromed, others gilt. They are calibrated from 1 to 15 and bear an enamelled town crest or regional emblem at the centre. The calibration and 'seaside souvenir' style indicate dates from the 1930s to the 1950s. Towns so far identified are Mevagissy, Leysdown on Sea, Nelson (New Zealand) and one bearing a Cornish pixie in relief.

Registers

Bestways, publishers of patterns and needlework magazines, offered a cardboard register which incorporated a 5″ rule, a needle gauge and a row and increase calculator. It dates from the 1930s, and was still being manufactured during WWII as on the reverse side of some examples is the legend 'A Handy Help for the War-Time Knitter'. Colours identified so far are buff and pale blue. It is fairly rare. A similar version, also rare, was made for Vicars.

A very rare rectangular compressed-cardboard gauge and register was made for Lazy Rainbow products. It is numbered from 2 to 16 and has a 3″ rule printed in green to the top with the words 'At A Glance'. The registers are in the form of revolving wheels at the back. The material is a composition typical of the 1930s but to date it accurately more needs to be known about this company.

In the 1930s Morralls offered a ruler-shaped 'measure, needle gauge, row indicator and line counter' called The Jesco Knit Glyde. It has a central clip to serve as

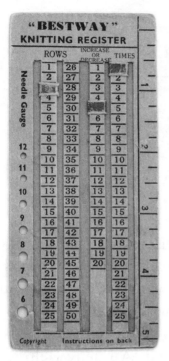

Both sides of a Bestway's cardboard register marked 'A Handy Help for the War-Time Knitter'.

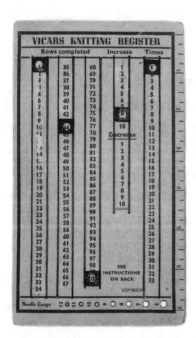

A similar register made for the haberdashery company, Vicars.

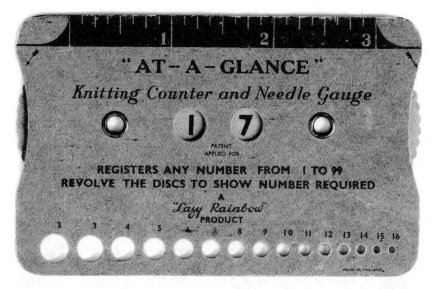

Brown compressed-cardboard register made for Lazy Rainbow
products. Interwar period.

a pattern marker and is in cream celluloid. It is fairly
rare.

It was quite common for large companies to offer items
made elsewhere. In Morrall's 1930s' trade catalogues are
several items in the '"MP" Handy Guide' range. The
most commonly found is a large rectangular register
and knitting guide. It has five rows with sliding knobs
for calculations. It is stoutly made in bronzed steel, has

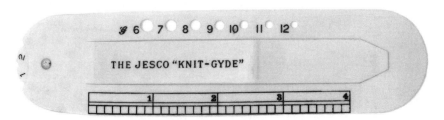

Celluloid Jesco Knit Glyde as advertised in Morrall's 1930s'
trade catalogues.

The "MP" Handy Guide as advertised in Morrall's 1930s'
trade catalogues. Bronzed steel.

seven needle sizes and a 4″ rule to the lower edge. Also
in the "MP" range is a fairly rare and fragile hinged
12″ rule in thin plastic or card. It has 16 needle sizes
and is also a 'Glove and Sock Measure'. (Illustrated on
colour plate 1.)

Women's Magazines

Magazines with a home crafts bias often gave free gifts with certain publications. Few meet the 1950s' date line, being products mainly of the 1960s and 1970s, but they do offer the collector an interesting field and are worth seeking out. The following gauges are the most commonly found: *Woman's Weekly, Woman's Own, Woman's Day, Woman, Woman's Realm, Woman's Illustrated, My Home and Family, Woman and Home, The People's Friend and Popular Crafts.*

Woman and Home free gift in blue plastic. 1950s.

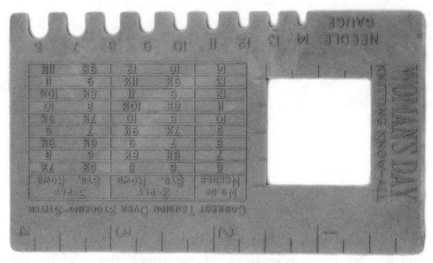

Woman's Realm and *Woman's Day* both offered these free gifts.
Found in pale blue and grey/green plastic. 1950s.

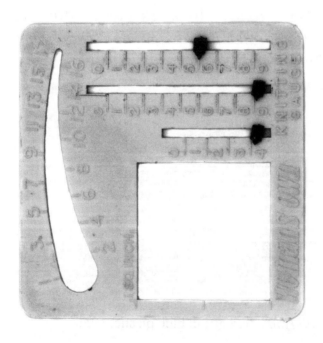

Small white
plastic gauge
and row
calculator
offered by
Woman's Own.
1950s

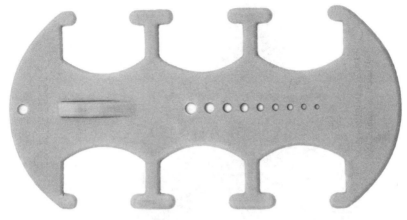

Yellow plastic 'Reel Tidi' presented free with
My Home and Family. 1950s

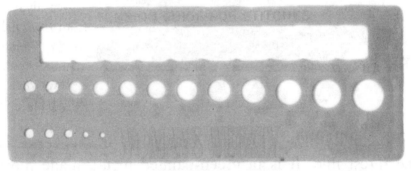

Yellow plastic tension guide and gauge offered by
Woman's Weekly. 1950s

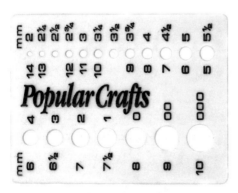

Modern gauge presented by
Popular Crafts.

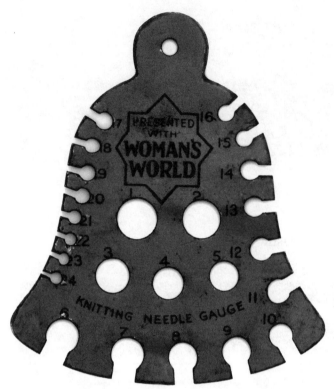

A rare bell give-away from *Woman's World*. Green-painted steel. Interwar period.

Woman's World – the only bell gauge in this series is the rarest find. It is in green-painted metal, made most probably by Morralls as it is identical to their pre-1933 Aero gauges.

Wool Ball Holders and Knitting Pin Boxes

(For illustrations, see colour plate 4.)

These interesting groups of knitting accessories, all featuring needle gauges, were made from the 1930s through to the 1950s by companies such as BEX, U-Plas and NB Ware.

Wool ball holders were designed to enclose the ball of wool, thus preventing it from soiling. They all have a cord or plastic ribbon at the top for keeping the holder on the wrist, and most have a needle gauge in the form of holes to the underside. Generally, those with cord wrist loops are the earlier as plastic ribbon was not in use until the mid 1940s.

Bakelite knitting pin boxes vary very much in size and colour but the important feature for the collector is the provision of a needle gauge. Some are located on the base; most on the top of the lid, and a few in the form of slots to the side of the lid. The narrow boxes are less common as they were made to take the finer needles used in the 1920s and 1930s and discarded when thicker yarns became more fashionable after WWII. All boxes made by the above companies will have imperial sizes only.

BEX holders and needle boxes were manufactured at the Halex factory at Hale End, near Manningtree, Essex. Halex was part of British Xylonite, a company with a history dating back to 1869 when it was pioneering the manufacture of celluloid. In 1935 they amalgamated with the Distillers Company to form BX Plastics and BEX Ware was born. In the 1960s the company was bought by Union Carbide, renamed Bakelite Industrial Plastics and moved to Birmingham.

BEX wool ball holders have a slightly domed lid which is impressed with a flower design. Set artistically in the flower centres are holes for the yarn and the cord handles. Colours seen so far are green and tan, but more colours are likely. They are fairly uncommon.

BEX knitting needle boxes vary in size. Slender 12″ boxes, found so far in pale green and pale blue, have the gauge in the form of slots to the side of the lid. The lids are marked 'Knitting Needles' and some examples are delicately painted with flowers. Whether the decoration is the result of enthusiastic amateurs or a cottage craft is not known. A wider 15″ version of this 'side gauge' type has been found in pink.

Wide 12″ BEX boxes are similarly marked on the lid but have the needle gauge to the centre. Colours so far identified are: forest green, olive green, maroon and pale blue. A wider range is likely. A good selection of these boxes can still be found.

NB Ware wool ball holders are fairly plentiful. They are dome shaped with ridged sides similar to a skip beehive. Examples with plastic ribbon handles date from the mid 1940s to the 1950s, but knitters remember earlier holders, probably with cord handles. They are found in a good range of colours: red, pale green, pink, sky blue, lilac and many more. They were manufactured by NB Mouldings, a company established in 1932 in the Holloway district of London. It was then known as Junction Moulds and Tools as their factory was housed in an old bus station. In 1948 they moved to a site in Tavistock Street, Dunstable, where they made goods for the motor car, electronics, cosmetics, domestic, boatbuilding and haberdashery industries. The company was sold to Osprey in the early 1990s and moved to Leyton Buzzard.

Little so far is known of the U-Plas company, but their pretty acorn-shaped wool ball holders are hard to find. Their plastic ribbon handles give them a post-WWII date. So far only a green version has been identified but other colours are likely.

Collectors will find various unbranded boxes with knitting pin gauges. Most are made of petroleum-based plastic and seem to date from the 1960s.

Australian Boxes

(For illustrations, see colour plate 2.)

A group of knitting pin boxes was made in Australia by Continental Plastics Pty Ltd in Melbourne. The material used is petroleum-based plastic and they all have a decorative lid moulded with a ball of wool speared by two knitting pins. The needle sizes, stamped on the lid, range from 00 to 16, indicating, as does the material, a post-WWII date. Colours identified so far are lime green and turquoise blue. A white version of the same box appears with a coral pink base and 'Hoadley's' moulded on the lid. These contained Hoadley's chocolates.

Metric Gauges

By the time that knitting needle sizes became metric in 1975 gauges were becoming plainer. Novelty shapes gave way to simple rules and rectangles incorporating both imperial and metric sizes. Although far from exciting, these gauges do offer the collector some choice. For instance, Milward's rectangular gauges appear in both anodised aluminium and plastic. The rare find is a Milward aluminium gauge embossed in Braille. (p.35)

The companies, too, were changing. In 1973 Milwards became part of the Coats Patons Group and manufacturing was increased at the factories in India which had been established by Milwards to cope with the shortages following WWII. In 1983 both Morralls and Milwards became part of the Needle Industries, but manufacturing in the United Kingdom dwindled and finally disappeared in the early 1990s. Milward's name lingers only on items made abroad and Morrall's Aero trademark is now assigned to the German company, Rump & Prym. (p.30)

Modern gauges exist, although their function is

limited. Only knitters using steel, double-pointed and very old pins need to size them. However, examples made by Pony and Polysew (both made in India), Birch (Australia), and Ariel (Continental with English sizes) are worth seeking out and collectors of modern gauges will find some delightfully original American designs.

Bibliography

Books

Deem, Harry, *A Century of Achievement, the Laughton Story* (York: Ebor Press, 1960)

Donald, Joyce, *Long Crendon, a Short History* (Long Crendon Preservation Society, 1983)

Harvey, Michael, *Patons – a Story of Hand Knitting* (Ascot: Springwood Books, 1985)

Henry Milward & Sons, *A Guide Through Washford Mills* (Birmingham, 1898)

Katz, Sylvia, *Early Plastics* (Princes Risborough: Shire Publications Ltd, 1994)

Lawson, Tom J., *Charles Horner of Halifax* (Leicester: GML Publishing, 2002)

Lee, Bernard T., *The Personal Reminiscences of a Needlemaker* (Devon: Merlin Books, 1986)

Rollins, John G., *The History of Redditch* (Phillimore & Co. Ltd, 1984)

Rutt, Richard, *The History of Handknitting* (London: B. T. Batsford Ltd, 1987)

Shrimpton and Page, *Notes on a Decayed Needleland* (Redditch: *Redditch Indicator*, 1897)

Documents

Assignment of the Goodwill and Business of Henry Walker, 27th November 1877. (In private hands, but, thanks to the Forge Mill Needle Museum, Redditch is available for study.)

Index